PASSION

&

PEACE

Lucille Morgan

First Printed in United Kingdom 2023

Published by Conscious Dreams Publishing
www.consciousdreamspublishing.com

Edited by Daniella Blechner

Typeset by Oksana Kosovan

Instagram: @luci_lucid_writes

Cover Art: Nancy Pitre Art
Instagram: @nancypitre.art

Photos: Kevin Ryan

ISBN: 978-1-915522-11-5

DEDICATION

To my mother and father—
for all the things you did right;
my deepest love & gratitude

Who stole my memory?
The thief is time
I was holding on
To the fragment
Of a passing rhythm
Taken away
Leaving a blur and haze
I stumbled
From illusion to fakery
Searching for the real
Give me back time
I want to remember
Who I was
In that time
And space
Long ago

I fell in love with a stranger
I thought it was
Beautiful
Everything
Forever
His ego smiled
Mine complied
I fell in love with a stranger
Who had expectations
Ambitions
Of bringing me down
Tapping into my fears
I fell in love with a stranger
And his darkness
It obscured
Distorted
My light

Half my mind
Half my heart
Half measures
Half empty
Half sad
Half fairy tale
Half lie
Half lost
Half a home
Half a life
Half of me
With you
Could never be
Whole

Wholeness
I sought
In tunnels
Corridors
Nooks
In there
I found
The broken
And unholy
I found others
Searching
For their missing pieces
In fear
We tried
To fuse our parts
Together
But they did not
Fit

Things
Rings
Glistening
Wedding
Happening
Fearing
Birthing
Dreaming
Despairing
Freeing
Weeping
Changing
Suffering
Calming
Enlightening
Uplifting
Loving
Listening
Hoping
Coping
Amazing
Blessing

Sporadic thoughts
Restless emotions
Melancholy musings
Chaos and confusion
Verve and vulnerability
Are my heart's calling
To come home

Depression
Is an expression
Of my distorted interior
A place that my soul
Oversees
But cannot intervene
The tragi-comedy unfolds
I as the player
And witness
The bearer
Of heaviness
I notice
When the lightness comes
I stand
On the edge of happiness

Sailing
Floating
On a sea
Of thoughts
Feelings rage
Waves toss
My weak vessel
I calm
Waters Subside
I notice the damage
Holes
That let the pain in
Sinking
I despair
I repair
My belief
My strength
And sail
To peace

Thoughts
I can sit
Stare at
Witness
At the dark
Under belly
Of disenchantment
Disaffection

Thoughts
That once held me
In an iron grip
No more concentrated
Diluted
Unstable
Gossamer weeds
In my mind

These parts of me
Now healthier
Less chaotic
And put together
To avoid collision
With the foe
Ego

Moments missed
Could have
Been hugged
And kissed
Absconder
Cold
Indefinable
Deserter
Inhuman
Heaven's disguise
Destiny's choice
Mental wounds
Damage of soul
He left a hole
A carefully kept
Book of secrets
My biological seed
Careless of my need
On Father's day
I remember
The challenge
Of overcoming

You're my peace
And the battle
You're my passion
And the wrath
You're the calm
And the chaos
You're the height
Of my joy
And the depth
Of my pain
You're my adventure
Most treacherous peak
You're my challenge
And triumph
You're my blood
Pulsing in my veins
You're my opening
To a new world
And my closure
On the past
You are
Every thing
Every place
Every one
Is you

I am brave enough
To ask
You
Anything
In the throw away moment

I can
Speak
And say
What I want
In the throw away moment
I can dance
Without judgement
Tripping me up

When the moment
Matters
I go back
and forth
In and out
of my shell
to hide
and expose
my beautiful parts

Sweet nothings
Turn into
Sweet somethings
This hardness
Meeting softness
It is anything
We make it out to be
Somethings
warm me
Somethings
Leavc me cold

Even now
When youth is long past
I feel
The freshness of ambition

Even now
Looking into love filled eyes
I feel
the emptiness of love mis-spent

Even now
When I stand proud
I feel
The smallness of the world

Even now
Bathed in sunshine
I recall
the chill of deep winter

Even now
When long held dreams are realised
I fall
into the abyss and weep

Destiny's deliveries
Are questionable
I did not ask
For troubles
In this size
The good bits
Came in the wrong colours
Love was a bit too tight
Frustration was extra large
Happiness was damaged
Peace was stained
Do I get a refund
Or can I send them back?

Let me
Fall in love
With your darkness
Then I will
Never be afraid
That you'll
Let me down
Leave me hanging

Betrayal
Is easy
When you sleep
With it
Every night
Pain is
Less damaging
When it's
Welcomed
As a guest

My heart
May greet you
As the enemy
My soul
Knows love
In your darkness

Between night and day
Lives
Wreckage and peace

Between day and night
is
Damage
Chaos
Condemnation
Storms
Unrest

Between day and night
I find
Myself

Make a moment
For me
so precious
It bring tears

Make a moment
That I can
Hold on to
And block
The sadness

Make a moment
To sustain
Nourish me
In the greyness
Of cloud filled skies

Make a moment
For me
To treasure
And shine
In your eyes

My doubts
Debilitate

My temper
Tightens

My ego
Swells

My patience
Peters out

My mind
Muddles

Regrets
Run riot

Time harnessed
And directed
On me

Peace
At last

Can a small ego
Take on the world?
Perhaps not alone
If our egos
marry
It could
get crowded
Or powerful
That would make us
Unstoppable

That is a world
Large
and
humble enough
For us
To fit into

Come up the hard way
Looked for a soft
Way out
The path was
Crooked
Broken
Painful
Yet still
I walked it
Was there
A gentler way?
Perhaps
But it was
Not mine

I'm done with the balcony
And shining from the east
I'm done with searching
For a dashing suitor
I'm done with feuds and swords
Meetings at midnight
I'm done with
Passion overtaking reason
I'm done with the hopelessness
Of youthful yearnings
I'm done with the helplessness
Of being in love
I'm done with drinking
Your poison kisses
I'm done with the sacrifice
Of my soul
I'm done with
This tragi-comedy
Too much Romeo
Not enough Juliet
End of the scene

On this journey
Of life
I learned
And loved
Art
Architecture
Literature
Music
Dance
People
The solid
And abstract
I learned
Appreciation
For sunlight
A butterfly's wing
The smell of the earth
The taste of the ocean
The feel of your skin
These distractions
Diversions
Overloaded
My sense
Of self

Words are powerful
As strong as actions
Your choice of words
Reveals
The beauty and ugliness
Of character
Hard and soft words
Words that bruise and bless
Words leave marks and cracks
In relationships
Words crown
Words crucify
They make me the queen
And you the king
That we know ourselves to be

OTHER BOOKS BY LUCILLE MORGAN

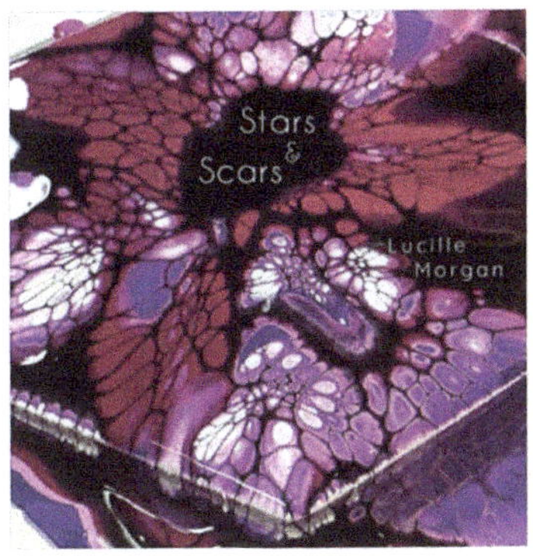

We are human and imperfect, but the world presses us to be something else. *Stars & Scars* is an exploration of that 'something else'. Thorny thoughts that make us uncomfortable for the tiny truths they contain. This is an invitation to delve deeper into the discomfort zone.

ABOUT THE AUTHOR

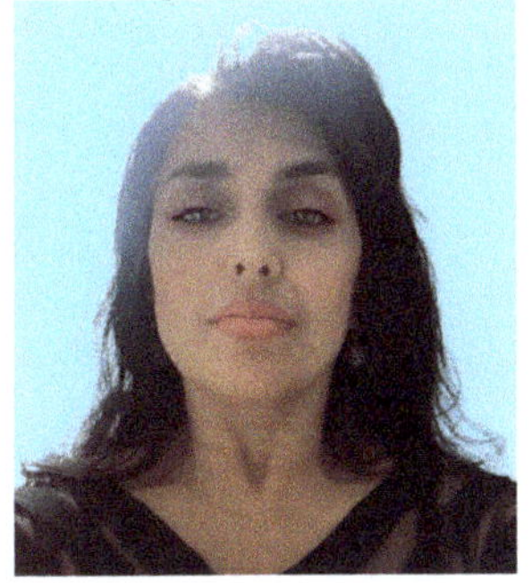

Lucille Morgan is a writer of prose poetry and fiction.
This is her second book.
Lucille lives in London with her children.

Milton Keynes UK
Ingram Content Group UK Ltd.
UKHW020649010823
426137UK00010B/14

9 781915 522115